What Is Crate Training?

"Why are all your dogs in those jails?" someone once asked when first visiting my home.

"Those aren't jails," I laughed. "They're crates. Check them out. Are my dogs acting like they're in prison?"

"Well, no," she said.

If my dogs were in "jail," they had to be the happiest prisoners on the cell block! One Labrador was wagging wildly, his tail thumping the crate sides while he slurped up the inside of a food-stuffed toy. My shy Shetland Sheepdog calmly eyed the visitor from the back of his crate, taking comfort at the door between them. My Papillon danced a brief joyful greeting at the crate door and then resumed the thorough task of nesting his blanket.

"I can't believe you have your dogs in these crates, but they seem perfectly fine with it," the visitor said. I understood her puzzlement. To someone not familiar with them, crates could be baffling. Why put your dog in a box?

"Think of them as playpens for dogs," I explained. "A playpen keeps a baby safe. She can have her toys in there, as well as comfy blankets. Parents use the playpen to keep a baby safe from harm, especially when they have to pay attention to other things, like fixing dinner or answering the phone. If a baby is confined to her playpen, she can't get into trouble. It's a tool parents use until she's old enough to behave and be safe with less supervision. Crating my dogs? Same concept!"

Crate Training Defined

Crate training is the act of teaching your animal to enter his enclosure and enjoy spending time in it.

A crate trained dog is one who has learned to enter his enclosure and enjoy spending time there.

The first time you bring home a crate, you wouldn't expect to just say, "Kennel up!" with Fido dashing right in and making himself at home. He probably won't have a clue what you want. Although he may be interested in this big box you brought him, he could just as easily interpret it as another piece of furniture rather than a cozy den. You need to teach him what you want.

Quick & Easy Crate Training

Crate
Training

Quick & Easy Crate Training

Project Team
Editor: Stephanie Fornino
Copy Editor: Carl Schutt
Design: Patricia Escabi
Cover Design: Candida M. Tómassini
Series Design: Mary Ann Kahn

T.F.H. Publications
President/CEO: Glen S. Axelrod
Executive Vice President: Mark E. Johnson
Publisher: Christopher T. Reggio
Production Manager: Kathy Bontz

T.F.H. Publications, Inc.
One TFH Plaza
Third and Union Avenues
Neptune City, NJ 07753

Printed and bound in China
08 09 10 11 12   3 5 7 9 8 4

ISBN   978-0-7938-1003-1

Library of Congress Cataloging-in-Publication Data
Anderson, Teoti.
Quick & easy crate training / Teoti Anderson.
p. cm.
Includes index.
ISBN 0-7938-1003-5 (alk. pap
1. Dogs-Training. 2. Crates. I. Title: Quick and easy crate training. II. Title.
SF431.A52 2005
636.7'0887–dc22
2005012985

This book has been published with the intent to provide accurate and authoritative information in regard to the subject matter within. While every reasonable precaution has been taken in preparation of this book, the author and publisher expressly disclaim responsibility for any errors, omissions, or adverse effects arising from the use or application of the information contained herein. The techniques and suggestions are used at the reader's discretion and are not to be considered a substitute for veterinary care. If you suspect a medical problem, consult your veterinarian.

The Leader In Responsible Animal Care For Over 50 Years! ®
www.tfh.com

Table
of Contents

What Is a Crate?

A crate is a rectangular cage made of a variety of sturdy materials (such as wire or molded plastic) used to keep an animal confined.

The biggest mistake people make in using crates is skipping the training part. If you put your dog in a crate and shut the door and leave him right off the bat, he'll be confused. He could even end up fearing his new den. To prevent this, I've outlined a training program in this book that you can use to teach your dog that his crate is a comfortable, fun place for him to stay.

Advantages of the Crate

Dogs are den animals. Have you ever noticed your dog curling up underneath your coffee table? Maybe snuggling under your bed covers? These actions make them feel comfortable and safe, and a crate takes advantage of their denning instinct.

Crates have many advantages for you as a dog owner as well. An important consideration is that they keep your dog safe. If your dog is in his crate, he's not chewing things that can hurt him. If you ever have to confine your dog due to health reasons, it's a lot easier if your dog is crate trained. Crates also can significantly help your housetraining efforts, because most dogs will not eliminate in their dens.

Have your friends or family started giving you excuses for not stopping by? If your bouncy puppy is in his crate instead of mauling your guests, you may enjoy having visitors again. Crates are also great for traveling, keeping your dog safe while in the car and while in the hotel room. Once you've reached your destination, the crate becomes a familiar, comforting den to your canine.

Responsibilities

As a responsible dog parent, it is your job to keep your dog safe. If your dog is in a crate, he won't have access to things that can hurt him.

Common Crate Myths

Crates have been used for a long time with great success, but there are still some old-fashioned ideas lurking out there that sometimes sour people's perceptions. Here are some common myths, along with the real scoop!

1. Crates are cruel.

A crate is a tool. You can use it for harm or for good, just as you can use a hammer to hurt someone or to build something useful. Any tool can be misused. If you put a dog in a crate 20 hours out of every day, and that dog never received any exercise or affection outside of the crate, then yes, the use of the crate would be cruel. If you put a dog in a crate that was too small, or put lots of dogs in one crate so that they didn't have enough room, then yes, the use of the crate would be cruel. If your dog eliminated in his crate and you never cleaned it, then yes, the use of the crate would be cruel. Unfortunately, there will always be some people who use tools improperly. But let's not throw the baby out with the bath water!

When introduced and used properly, a crate is a wonderful tool that can keep your dog safe from harm. This book will teach you how to use a crate effectively so that both you and your dog benefit!

2. Confining a dog in a room will work just as well as crating.

While some dogs do fine in a room (such as a kitchen, bathroom or laundry room) rather than a crate, it doesn't work well for every dog. In a room, your dog may still have access to things that can hurt him. One day your puppy will be fine, but the next day he'll round off every cabinet corner or discover the toilet paper roll and redecorate the room. Some dogs will even chew holes in the wall! The destruction you find when you get home will be a major inconvenience and possibly expensive to fix, but that's not as serious as the damage your dog can do to himself. Dogs can eat things that hurt them. Splinters from cabinets can slice their gums. Wads of paper or sheetrock can get stuck in your dog's intestinal tract, requiring emergency surgery. And although puppies are more prone to chewing, even adult and senior dogs get into things they shouldn't. Senior dogs with no history of destructive behavior have been known to start chewing later in life, sometimes with tragic consequences.

Another challenge is confinement itself—some dogs are great escape artists. They'll jump over baby gates or even manage to go through them. Some scratch doorways to ribbons. And once your dog realizes he can get loose, it can be difficult to keep him confined. He's learned that once he escapes, your entire house becomes his playground.

If you are trying to housetrain your dog, confining him in his crate will be more effective than putting him in a larger room. Most dogs will not eliminate in their crates, which they perceive as their dens. If you give him a larger den, he can just potty in a corner and stay away from his mess all day. This will not teach him to avoid eliminating indoors. A crate gives him less room, so he will be less likely to potty in it. You'll be giving him fewer opportunities to practice eliminating inside and more

Although confinement in a room may work for some dogs, a crate offers better safety and a greater chance of successful housetraining.

If you crate train your dog properly, he will enjoy his crate and view it as a safe den.

opportunities to practice eliminating outside. The more he practices, the better he will get.

3. If I crate my dog, I'm a bad doggy parent.

Don't you hate it when guilt whispers in your ear? It would be great if none of us had to work and could spend all day every day with our dogs to keep them safe and occupied. However, many dog owners have to work and leave their dogs during the day. Also, people have to leave their homes at one point or another without taking Fido along. That's just life. If we want canines to be a part of our lives, both species have to adapt to make it work.

Your dog will adapt better than you will. You'll head off to work, thinking you're a miserable human being leaving your furry kid locked in a dungeon. Meanwhile, your dog will chew on his toys and contentedly curl up and nap until you get home. Who's the one suffering? You are! If you introduce and use a crate properly, your dog will love his safe den.

If you feel guilty, learn how to use the crate properly. Give your dog tons of attention and exercise outside the crate when you're home. Remember all the good reasons for using the crate in the first place, and don't let your family or friends make you feel like an evil doggy parent. (Give them a copy of this book so they can be educated about crates, too!) You'll enjoy peace of mind, and so will your dog.

Preparing the Crate

A good crate training plan starts with preparation. This includes choosing a crate and setting it up properly. By taking some time to do these things carefully, you'll ensure a positive training experience for your dog, as well as much less hassle for you!

Choosing a Crate

Years ago, dog owners had very little choice when it came to crates, as there were only a few types on the market. If you wanted a crate, you pretty much got the same one as your neighbor. As more and more people learned the value of crate training, though, the demand for different types of crates grew. Companies rushed to meet the demand. Today, there is a tremendous variety of crates from which to choose, and this can be quite confusing. How do you know which one to buy?

Types of Crates

Some crates are better suited for certain purposes. Some crates are better for adult dogs than puppies, for example, while other crates are better for certain breeds. Let's review the most common types of crates and see which one will best fit you and your dog.

Crate Type	Best Uses	Features	Consider:
Plastic	• Puppy training • Adult dog training • Confinement • Housetraining • Travel	• Sturdy. • Provide limited view. • Can come apart for cleaning and transition to dog bed. • Usually less expensive then others.	• Nuts and screws may come lose. • Some dogs will chew plastic. • Some crates have raised sections on bottoms that can be awkward to clean. • Some do not fold up for storage/travel (check brands). • May have to purchase larger crates as puppy grows.
Wire	• Puppy training • Adult dog training • Confinement • Housetraining • Travel	• Sturdy. • Good for strong chewers. • Provide good view. • Many fold up for storage/travel. • Bedpan pulls out for cleaning. • Some feature dividers for growing puppies.	• Some space between wires may be too big relative to dog's size, which could catch paws and cause injury. • If dog gets sick, can overspill bedpan. • Usually more expensive than others.
Canvas	• Adult dog training • Confinement • Travel	• Lightweight. • Easy to set up/take down.	• Not good for chewers. • Surface not as easy to clean as others.
Soft-Sided Carriers	• Travel	• Lightweight.	• Best for small dogs only. • Surface not as easy to clean as others.

Plastic Crates

Plastic crates are good for training your puppy or adult dog, and they work well for confinement purposes, for housetraining, and for travel. They come in a variety of sizes, and they are sturdy, so they can be good for confining active dogs. They're also usually less expensive than other kinds.

If you have a large breed puppy, the crate that fit him when he was young may not when he is an adult.

If you have a large breed puppy, take note: You may find you have to purchase different-sized plastic crates as your dog grows. If your puppy is in a crate that's too big, he could still find it tempting to potty in there. You could purchase a crate suitable for his adult size and try to make it smaller by blocking a portion of it with a box or other object, but your dog could end up chewing whatever it is you decide to use.

Many plastic crates come in two parts—the top and bottom are held together with nuts and screws, and you can take the pieces apart for easy cleaning. This comes in handy, because some plastic crates have raised areas on them instead of being completely smooth. These can cause dirt to be easily trapped in the crate, which makes it awkward to clean unless you completely take the crate apart.

Making a Dog Bed Base

A plastic crate's take-apart feature can also serve as a transition for your dog. If he graduates from the crate, you can use the bottom as a familiar dog bed base.

Flying With Fido

If you want to fly anywhere with your dog, most airlines approve plastic crates. Some plastic crates even have wheels on them so you can glide Fido through the airport easily. Always check with an individual airline to get its specific requirements.

If you choose a plastic crate held together with nuts and screws, it's important to check that the screws are tight on a regular basis. Some dogs jostle around in their crates and can gradually loosen them. You don't want the nuts and screws falling out and Fido getting hold of them. (Try explaining that to your veterinarian as you look at the x-rays!)

Plastic crates generally offer your dog less view of his environment. Some dogs find that to be a comfort. If you have a very shy dog, for example, the enclosure of a plastic crate may make him feel safer. If you have a reactive dog—one who barks at movement, sounds, etc.—this may also be a good choice because it'll be harder for him to see the things that trigger his barking.

Some dogs like to chew their crates, and the plastic can end up with rough edges. If you have a plastic crate and a chewer, try spraying a chew deterrent on the parts your dog has taken a fancy to munching. These sprays are available at local pet stores, department stores, and online pet retailers.

Some people want their crates to be colorful, and plastic crates do come in a variety of colors. Keep in mind that with some brands, the color depends on the size of the crate. For example, the large crate may only come in blue, and the medium crate may always be beige.

If you want to put your plastic crate away for storage, or if you want to travel with it, it can be a bit bulky. If you get one that comes apart, you can store the top in the bottom, but it will still take up space. Some brands do fold up, so if this is a feature you need, check out the different options available.

Wire Crates

Like plastic crates, wire crates are good for training your puppy or adult dog, and they work well for confinement, housetraining, and travel. They come in a variety of sizes, and they also come in different finishes—there's pewter, plain wire, silver and gold finishes, and more. The ones with epoxy coating come in a variety of colors and are resistant to rust. These crates are sturdy and are good for strong chewers. Wire crates are usually more expensive than other kinds.

The mesh on wire crates varies with each brand. Some have wide openings, while some have small openings. Be sure to get one with small holes in relation to your dog's size so that your dog won't catch a paw in the mesh and possibly hurt himself.

These crates feature a solid plastic or metal bedpan on the bottom to catch accidents and messes. To clean it, you just pull the bedpan out, clean it off, and slide it back in. If your dog gets sick and suffers vomiting or diarrhea, however, do know that it could overspill the pan, go through the wire openings, and onto your floor. Hopefully this won't happen often!

Wire crates come in a variety of sizes and finishes and are good for strong chewers.

Preparing the Crate   15

Many wire crates come with dividers. This means that if you have a small puppy who will grow to be a large dog, you can buy one crate to fit your puppy when he's an adult. You just move the divider as he grows. This will limit the amount of room he has and help with your housetraining efforts. If he is in a smaller area, he will be less likely to potty in his crate.

Wire crates give your dog a good view of his environment. If he likes to see what's going on around him, a wire crate will let him soak up the sights. If your dog is shy, however, this much "open space" may be intimidating. Or if you have a very reactive dog, you may want to restrict his ability to see things that could trigger barking or agitated behavior. Some companies make crate covers for wire crates; these can be helpful if you want to restrict your dog's view or if you want the crate to better fit in with your home's decor. Crate covers are made of fabric and drape over the crate's sides. Some companies even make matching crate bedding for your dog's comfort!

Many wire crates fold up "suitcase-style" for easy storage and travel. These usually feature handles you can use to carry them. If you're having company over and need to move Fido's den to another room, this is a handy feature. Also, if you're traveling with your dog, this feature makes it easy to take Fido's den on your trip.

Canvas Crates

Canvas crates are good for confinement and travel. They're also good for adult dogs who are past the chewing phase. If you have a puppy or a chewer, though, canvas crates make very expensive chew toys! Canvas is just not as sturdy as other materials, so be sure to use this kind of crate only with dogs who are not destructive.

Canvas material can be harder to clean than plastic or metal, as it's a fabric. Some brands do feature removable, machine-washable covers.

Canvas crates come in a variety of colors, and they are very lightweight, even in the larger sizes. Almost anyone can carry them, which is great for people who might have difficulty lugging around heavier crates. It also makes them extremely convenient for trips because they set up easily and fold down to a small size for space efficiency. Some even come in tent shapes made especially for camping.

If you compete with your dog and travel to agility, flyball, rally-o, or obedience trials, a canvas crate could be your favorite dog accessory.

Soft-Sided Carriers

Soft-sided carriers are great for travel. They are geared toward small dogs, and they usually feature a shoulder strap so you can carry Fluffy conveniently. Some are plain and look like business luggage, while others are worthy of any fashion designer's accessory line. Because they can range from practical to trendy, the prices vary.

Some airlines have approved certain brands as suitable for air travel. Always check with your specific airline to make sure your carrier will be acceptable.

Soft-sided carriers are geared toward small dogs and are perfect for travel.

Soft-sided carriers can be harder to clean than other materials, as they are usually made of canvas or fabric. They are best for dogs who are not chewers.

Other Types of Crates

Some companies have come out with designer materials for their crates, like rattan or even sleek metals. If you are hesitant about adding a crate to your home because you think they are unattractive, then these designer crates may be the perfect solution. Just be sure to match the material to your dog—if you have a puppy chewer, for example, then rattan would not be a good choice. This doesn't mean that you have to sacrifice looks for function forever, though. You can start with a more durable crate and work up to one of the more fashionable options as your puppy matures.

Crate Size

What size crate you choose will depend on what you want to use it for.

Housetraining

If you want to use a crate for housetraining, then it should just be big enough for your dog to stand up, stretch out, and turn around in. Anything bigger and he will be able to eliminate in his crate and stay high and dry the rest of the time, which will make it harder for him to learn bladder and bowel control.

Getting a small crate may seem cruel at first. But if you're following a good housetraining program, your dog can gradually earn more room the more he learns what you expect of him.

General Confinement

If your dog is already housetrained and you need a crate to confine him when you can't supervise him, then get a crate with plenty of room for him to stretch out in and relax.

Keep in mind that when crate companies associate breed recommendations with their crate sizes, they're using common sizes for those breeds. If you have a super-sized Shetland Sheepdog, then the crate labeled for Shelties may actually be too small for your dog. Try to go by weight rather than breed.

There are advantages and disadvantages to keeping two puppies in the same crate.

It's not a bad idea to give your housetrained dog a super-sized crate. If you have a Yorkshire Terrier who is housetrained and just needs confinement when you're away from home, then feel free to buy a crate designed for a Labrador Retriever. Just choose one that is safe enough for his little paws and parts!

Travel

If you have limited space in your vehicle, it can be tempting to get a crate that barely fits your dog to save space. Don't. Your dog should be able to stand up, stretch out, and relax in his travel crate. Those long rides can be uncomfortable if he's cramped and has to curl up in a little ball to fit. And as your dog gets older, those bones and joints will get creakier, so giving him ample room to travel will help keep him in shape for your adventures.

Where to Find a Crate

You can find crates at your local pet store or online pet retailer. Some major discount department stores and discount shopping warehouses also carry crates. The same crate can be available at a wide range of prices depending on the store, so you can save money with a little research.

Doubling Up

 Some people get littermates or two young puppies and want to keep them together in a large crate.

Advantages:

- You only have to buy one crate.
- The puppies can entertain each other when they're in the crate.
- You may feel less guilty leaving them in the crate if they have each other for company.

Disadvantages:

- You'll need to buy a large enough crate to accommodate two growing puppies, so it may end up being big enough so they feel comfortable enough to eliminate in there. This will undo your housetraining efforts.
- Your puppies may end up becoming overly dependent on each other and bond more with each other than with you.
- As your puppies get older, they could start squabbling.
- If they ever have to be separated due to illness or injury, you'll need two crates.

You can sometimes find good deals on used crates. If you buy one, be sure it's in good condition and appropriate for your specific dog. For example, if it's an epoxy-coated wire crate, how is the coating holding up? Are there patches missing or showing rust? You don't want your dog licking rust! Are the wire holes in the mesh more suitable for a Collie than your Cairn Terrier? Look over a used crate as you would a used car. After all, it's going to be holding your precious cargo. You don't want to save a few dollars up front, only to spend more later patching up your dog's injuries.

Setting Up Your Crate

Once you find the perfect crate for your dog, it's time to set it up in your home. You'll need to make some decisions about where you should place it and what, if anything, you should put in it. Your choices will depend on your lifestyle, as well as your individual dog.

Where to Put the Crate

A common question people have is "Where do you put the crate?" It's important to put the crate in an area of your home where your family will spend the most time. If you set up the crate in a laundry room or spare bedroom, away from your family's daily activities, your dog will feel left out. He'll also be less likely to bond with family members, because he'll be kept isolated from them.

Your dog is a pack animal, and your family is his pack. Your dog wants to be with you, even if he's in his crate. By putting the dog in the middle of your life, you're making your dog a part of that life. Keep in mind that dogs who feel lonely will often whine, bark, or howl to get attention. They're not being spiteful—they're upset!

Put your dog's crate in an area of the home where your family spends the most time.

They're trying to tell you they miss you and want to be closer to you. This is why it's so important to put the crate right in the heart of things, because this setup will allow your dog to see what's going on around him and feel your presence nearby.

What about when it's time for bed? It's up to you whether you want to put the crate in your bedroom. If you do, it's handy to have a crate that moves easily or to just get another crate for that room. Generally, your dog will want to be with you. But if you don't want your dog in the bedroom, he'll survive just fine.

What's confusing to a dog is when you can't make up your mind. For example, he won't understand if you start in the bedroom for a couple of weeks, then kick him out for a while, then let him back in. Just decide what you want and be consistent. He'll learn his crate routine much easier that way.

It's also important to keep the crate clear from anything your dog could pull inside. Some dogs have been known to drag neighboring tablecloths, electrical wires, and other assorted dangerous items into their crates if they can reach them.

What to Put in the Crate
What you put in your dog's crate depends a lot on your dog.

Bedding
You may be tempted to put a soft, cushiony bed in the crate for your puppy, but that could prove disastrous if your pup shreds it to bits. Some dogs will actually eat bedding, which could get stuck in their digestive tracts and require emergency surgery. Some won't eat it but will tear it to ribbons and leave a huge mess. It may seem harsh to put a puppy in a crate without a bed, blanket, or even a towel to make it more comfortable, but if you have a destructive puppy, don't take that chance. It's far crueler to let your dog get hurt!

As your puppy grows up and becomes less destructive, you can try putting softer things in his crate. You can leave him in there with a durable bed for 15 minutes, then 30 minutes, then 60 minutes, and then work up to where you're convinced he won't destroy it if you're not there to stop him. Take your time, and keep in mind that some dogs simply never outgrow the chewing stage. This probably isn't what you wanted to read, but it's true. Not all dogs stop chewing as they become adults. Some dogs are perfectly content to shred things until they're senior citizens; it just depends on the individual dog.

If your dog is not able to have a bed in his crate, he'll be fine, unless he has a condition such as hip dysplasia or an injury that requires softer flooring. In that case, try finding a bed made especially for chewers. Test it, as some chewers are pretty persistent! You can spray it with a chew deterrent, which may keep your dog from munching on it. It's a good idea to talk to your veterinarian about what exactly your dog needs to be comfortable in the crate.

Toys

The crate should also have toys in it to occupy your dog's mind and body during his confinement. Be very careful about what kind of toys you leave with your dog while he's unsupervised.

Is your dog a shredder? Some dogs like to rip apart stuffed animals. Others will surgically remove the squeakers and then leave the rest of the stuffed animal alone. Still other dogs can have the same stuffed animal remain intact their entire lives. If your dog likes to tear things apart, don't leave toys in his crate that are easily destroyed. He could ingest parts of them, which could cause major medical problems.

Is your dog a power chewer? Does he go through dog bones like they're candy? Some dogs will nibble and nibble at a bone for weeks. Others act like canine chippers and pulverize them in minutes. If your dog goes through bones quickly, be sure to only leave bones in his crate that are very, very tough—Nylabone makes a few.

Do not leave toys with your dog he could get a paw caught in, and make sure they are big enough so he doesn't choke on them. If he's been working a dog bone and it's getting small enough for him to fit almost entirely in his mouth, it's time to throw it away. It's true that any toy you leave with your dog unsupervised could potentially cause a problem. However, by understanding your dog and how he treats his toys, and by doing your research and picking sturdy ones, you'll ensure a safer crate experience.

You should vary the toys you leave in your dog's crate so he doesn't grow bored with them. If your dog is surrounded by toys, he'll soon get used to all of them and lose interest. (It's like how we feel about satellite or cable television—there are hundreds of channels, but we keep clicking the remote looking for something to watch.) Rotate the toys so he feels there's a variety.

With any toy you choose to leave in the crate, be sure you don't only use it while he's being crated. For example, if you only give him a food-stuffed rubber toy in his crate when you leave for work, then he may start associating that toy with you leaving and not want it

Collars

anymore. You want your dog to love his toys, not dread them! So be sure to give a food-stuffed rubber toy at other times, when he's not going to be crated.

Food and Water

It's perfectly fine to feed your dog in his crate. If you are trying to housetrain your dog, however, I don't recommend leaving food in there for him to nibble on all day. Instead, you should set a schedule for regular meals. I recommend putting the food in there for about ten minutes, then taking it away until his next scheduled meal.

Dogs should have access to fresh water throughout the day. If your dog likes to play in his water, though, this can pose a challenge in a

Your individual dog's habits will help you determine whether or not to leave food and water in the crate.

crate. You don't always want to come home to a soggy puppy! Some dogs do fine when you place a water bowl in their crates, right on the floor. Some crates come with plastic water bowls that hook onto the crate door, which can work fine, too. But some dogs will upend water bowls, causing a mess. They may also chew on the plastic crate bowls. This will roughen the edges and could prove to be a hazard. Your dog could also swallow the plastic pieces he breaks off, which could cause some major medical problems.

If your dog constantly flips his water bowl or is a chewer, try a metal coop cup. These come in a variety of sizes, and you can find them at your local pet store or online pet retailer. (Sometimes you'll find them in the bird section, although many people use them for other animals.) These cups feature a ring that goes inside the crate door, which is secured with nuts and bolts outside the crate door. The bowl fits snugly inside the ring, and it's harder to flip over, because it's suspended from the crate door. Metal is also much less appealing as a chew toy, so your dog will be less likely to chew it up.

That said, there are still some dogs who will find a way to dislodge a coop cup and splash about happily like a duck until you get home. If you've tried everything and it hasn't worked, and you don't want a soggy dog, then leave the water out of the crate. If you do this, you must be sure you are keeping a realistic crate schedule for your dog and that he gets plenty of fresh water throughout the day at other times. Be sure his crate is not in an area where he could become overheated, too. If you make sure he's getting the hydration he needs at other times, then he should be fine with no water in his crate. If you're not sure how much water your dog needs, consult your veterinarian.

Taking the time to choose the right crate for your dog and set it up properly will help build a foundation for successful crate training. You have put a lot of thought into the home you chose for yourself—now you've worked to find the right den for your dog!

Introducing the Crate

You have the crate open and waiting for Fido to discover. But how long should your dog stay in there? What time frame is realistic for his age? Is there such a thing as too much time in the crate? Understanding these issues will help shape successful crate training sessions.

Setting a Schedule

Before you start crate training, you need to set a realistic schedule for how long your dog will stay in his crate.

Puppies

It is unrealistic to expect a young puppy to hold his bladder and bowels all day when you're at work. A young puppy has to have a midday break! You can hire a pet sitter to stop by during the day, ask one of your neighbors or friends to help you, or come home from work if you're able. But your young puppy simply can not hold it all day. Some puppies will try—and this can cause urinary tract infections and other kidney problems. Many will just give up and eliminate in their crates, which will set back your housetraining program significantly. The goal is for him to avoid eliminating in his den, but if he's confined too long, he'll have to potty. This will teach him to live near or in his mess, which can then become a very hard habit to break. Set yourself up for successful housetraining and a positive experience with the crate by setting a realistic schedule.

Sample Crate Schedule for Puppy, Owner Works Outside of Home

Here is a sample schedule for you to get an idea of how long a young puppy can be crated.

7:30 a.m.	Wake up and potty break.
7:40 a.m.	Feed puppy breakfast.
7:50 a.m.	Potty break. Put puppy in crate.
8:30 a.m.	Owner leaves for work.
12:30 p.m.	Neighbor gives puppy potty break.
12:40 p.m.	Neighbor gives puppy midday meal.
12:45 p.m.	Neighbor gives puppy potty break. Puts puppy in crate.
5:30 p.m.	Owner arrives home. Potty break.
6:30 p.m.	Potty break.
7:30 p.m.	Feed puppy dinner.
7:40 p.m.	Potty break.
9:00 p.m.	Potty break. Take away water so puppy can better hold bladder all night.
10:00 p.m.	Final potty break. Puppy goes in crate for the night.

In general, your puppy will need a midday break up until he's about six months old. This means he can be in his crate for about four to five hours at a stretch. Remember, the younger your puppy is, the more frequent potty breaks he will need. This can be a hassle if your work schedule is hectic or if your boss won't let you take a break for your dog. However, keep in mind that puppyhood doesn't last forever. If you properly train your puppy for the first six months, you will be setting yourselves up for long-term success.

When you set your schedule, try to stick to it every day as close as possible. If you set up a routine that works for both of you, your dog will be more consistent with his behavior.

Older Dogs

After reaching six months of age, most puppies are able to hold their bladders and bowels longer, depending on the individual dog. Ideally, you should offer a midday potty and exercise break. However, you may have to crate your dog if you work an eight-hour job. If you can continue the midday breaks, that's great! If not, crate your older puppy while you're at work, with an extra emphasis on proper exercise and attention outside the crate when you get home. Your dog does have needs you must meet to keep him physically, mentally, and emotionally fit.

If you have a 12-hour-a-day job or shift, then it's important to arrange for someone to come let your dog out for a potty and play break before you get home. Asking a dog to remain in his crate for 12 hours won't ruin all the training you've accomplished if it's an emergency or a rare occasion, but it's not healthy for your dog to do it every day. This is especially true if you have a very active breed, as this could cause emotional and behavioral issues. For example, a typical young Labrador Retriever who is cooped up for 12 straight hours is going to come out of his crate like a rocket. He'll be difficult to manage and unable to focus his attention. He's not doing this deliberately to make you angry. It's just that he hasn't had the mental and physical exercise he needs. And he won't get any better until those needs are met!

If your regular day will mean your dog must remain confined for more than eight or nine hours, then please find a way to give your dog a break during the stretch. Set a realistic schedule and you and your dog will be much happier and healthier!

Sample Crate Schedule for Older Dogs, Owner Works Outside of Home

Here is a sample schedule for a dog who is more than six months old.

7:30 a.m.	Potty break.
7:40 a.m.	Feed dog breakfast.
7:50 a.m.	Put dog in crate.
8:30 a.m.	Owner leaves for work.
5:30 p.m.	Owner arrives home. Potty break.
7:00 p.m.	Potty break.
7:30 p.m.	Feed dog dinner.
7:40 p.m.	Potty break.
10:00 p.m.	Final potty break. Dog goes in crate for the night if necessary.

With this schedule, there are less potty breaks. This is because an adult dog can physically hold his bladder and bowels better than a young puppy. As dogs get older, they become more dependent on routines; by sticking to your schedule as closely as possible, you'll fall into a pattern that works well for both of you.

Choosing a Cue

Decide what cue you want to use when your dog goes into his crate. You'll use this cue every single time. Some suggestions include "Go to kennel!" or "Kennel up!" It doesn't matter what cue you use, as long as you make sure that you (and your family) use the same cue for this specific action every time. If you say, "Go to kennel" but

Short and Sweet

your spouse says, "Kennel up!" it will be harder for your dog to learn what you both mean.

Introducing the Crate to a Puppy

Until approximately 16 weeks of age, puppies have a socialization period that can affect their view of the world for the rest of their lives. Any positive experiences they have during this time will have a great impact on them. If they learn that the world is a safe place and that people are friendly, then they have a better chance of growing up to be well-adjusted dogs. If they have negative experiences during this time, they can become shy or even aggressive.

Most puppies come to live with their humans between 8 and 12 weeks of age. (Puppies younger than 8 weeks of age have not finished learning valuable social lessons from their mother and siblings.) With puppies this age, it's more realistic to actually put the puppy in his crate rather than wait for him to go into it. This is because puppies have the attention spans of turnips! They may head for the crate and be distracted by lint 4 feet away. By making the crate experience fun for your puppy, you'll teach him

If you have to confine your dog for long periods of time, a play and potty break in the middle is necessary.

If you make the crate experience fun for your puppy, he'll learn to view it as a safe den.

that his crate is his safe den. You'll also help him to enjoy being confined for realistic amounts of time.

Step 1

First, set the stage so your puppy views his crate as a positive place. Keep the crate door open and get some delicious treats that your puppy likes. You can even use your dog's kibble breakfast for this exercise.

Next, show your puppy the treat and toss or place it in the crate. You may find you need to put the treats near the crate door at first. You can even leave a little trail of treats from the crate door toward the back of the crate. Don't shut the door behind him yet.

When your puppy goes in after the treat, praise him. Repeat this exercise several times over the course of a few hours.

Common Challenges

Remember, puppies have no attention spans. If you toss a treat in the crate and your puppy hears a noise outside that distracts him, he'll completely forget about the treat. You'll have to remind him. If he's not interested at all, try using different treats. Space the exercise out more so you're not overwhelming him.

Step 2

Pick up your puppy. (Be sure you do it carefully so he feels safe and secure.) Give your cue ("Go to kennel!" or whatever cue you chose), and gently place your puppy in his crate. Immediately give him a tasty treat and praise him. Then, shut the crate door for a few seconds and talk cheerfully to your puppy. Try not to say things like, "It's okay, baby, it's okay," because if you do, you're essentially telling him that things are not, in fact, okay. Don't reassure him as if something is wrong. Just happily tell him he's a good boy for being in his crate.

If your puppy should start pawing, whining, or barking at the crate door, don't talk to him at all. You will just be encouraging this behavior. It will be hard for you, but ignore him. If you don't, you'll undo all of your training efforts. Just wait until he calms down.

Open the crate door as long as your puppy is not crying, whining, barking, or pawing the crate door. Be calm and quiet when you do. This can be hard, but many people make the mistake of saying, "Yay! Good boy!" as their dog *leaves* the crate. This teaches a puppy that it's better to leave the crate than go into it. So save all your praise for this exercise for when your puppy is *in* the crate. When he gets out, just be matter-of-fact about it.

Repeat this exercise a couple of times, gradually

Give your puppy some toys to help him become accustomed to the crate.

Tips to Remember

The following are some tips to remember when helping your puppy become accustomed to his crate:

- Use your cue every time you put your puppy in his crate.
- Don't forget to give him a toy or two.
- When your puppy is outside the crate, be sure he's getting plenty of playtime, potty breaks, and nap opportunities.

increasing the amount of time your puppy is in his crate. You'll go from a few seconds to a few minutes to even longer periods of time. Your puppy will likely spend the night in his crate, so the more comfortable he is by the time night falls, the better you'll both sleep.

Step 3

After a few days of crate routine, it's time to teach your puppy to go into his crate on his own rather than you placing him there.

First, put a treat in your hand. Show it to your puppy and give him the cue "Go to kennel!" Then, use the treat in your hand to lure him into the crate. If he follows your hand into the crate, give him the treat when he gets into the crate and praise him. Do this several times a day. If he does not follow the treat lure into the crate, try using more tempting treats.

Introducing the Crate to an Older Dog

What if your puppy is past the socialization period and has never been in a crate? Or what if you just added an adult dog to your family who has never been confined in a crate? An older dog has had more experiences in life that could either give him a negative or positive impression of the world. If your dog has never been confined, it would be startling and perhaps traumatic for him if you tossed him in the crate and shut the door.

This is why it's important to go slowly with him so that he associates only good things with his new crate. The process will take a bit more time, but it will be worth the wait. If you push too fast, you could create a dog who is scared of his crate, and then you will have lost all of the crate's benefits.

Step 1

First, set the stage for the crate being a positive place. Keep the crate door open, and get some delicious treats that your dog likes. You can even use your dog's meals for this exercise.

Show your dog a treat and toss or place it in the crate. You may find that you need to put the treats near the crate door at first. You can even leave a little trail of treats from the crate door toward the back of the crate. Don't shut the door behind him yet.

When your dog goes in after the treat, praise him. Repeat this exercise until your dog is comfortably going into the crate for treats. This may take a day, or it may take a week, depending on the individual dog.

Step 2

Start feeding all of your dog's meals inside his crate. Here's how: Get his meal ready, put the bowl in the crate, and shut the door—with the dog outside the crate. Wait about five minutes for him to build up some anticipation, then let him in the crate with his

If you are crate training an adult dog, go slowly so that he associates only good things with his crate.

cue "Go to kennel!" (or whatever cue you've chosen). Let him eat his meal without shutting the door behind him.

Step 3

If your dog is now eagerly going into his crate, you are ready for Step 3. If he still resists, spend some more time on Steps 1 and 2. If you push your dog too fast, you will undo all of your hard work.

Get a treat in your hand. Show it to your dog and give him the cue "Go to kennel!" Then, use the treat in your hand to lure him into the crate. If he follows your hand, give him the treat when he gets into the crate and praise him. Do this several times a day. If he does not follow the treat lure into the crate, go back to Steps 1 and 2 for awhile, and then try again using better treats.

Now that your dog is happily going into his crate, start shutting the door for a few minutes and then let him out—but only if he's being quiet and not barking or pawing at the door. Always make sure he's behaving when you let him out, so he'll learn that good manners bring rewards.

Gradually increase the time your dog stays in his crate. Start with a few minutes, then a half-hour, then an hour. Make sure to give him plenty of breaks in between your crate training sessions.

When dogs don't like their crates, it's usually because people either have unrealistic schedules or have skipped this initial training. Understanding your dog's daily routine and offering a positive introduction to his den will make a huge difference in how your dog reacts to his crate. Remember, first impressions last a long time.

Crate Training:
Making Confinement Fun for Your Dog

Can you imagine leaving a human toddler alone in your living room while you head off to work? You would never dream of doing that! Leaving a puppy or young dog loose in your home while you're away is the same thing. While you're out of the house, they'll find things to amuse themselves—things that are rarely what you would have chosen for them.

When dogs (especially puppies) are left to roam around the house unsupervised, they can get into trouble. They can also get hurt. This is where crate training can save the day, your belongings, and your dog.

When Confinement Is Necessary

By making confinement fun for your dog, you are keeping him safe and comfortable until you can supervise him to prevent bad things from happening. The following situations may require you to confine your dog to preserve the health and happiness of your dog, the people he comes in contact with, and your possessions.

Chewing

Dogs can destroy things that have value to you, like your expensive shoes, your daughter's beloved teddy bear, or your husband's prized baseball card collection. Are they doing it to spite you? Not likely. Dogs are built to chew things—just look at those teeth! Dogs chew for many reasons:

- They're teething. At around four months of age, a puppy's adult teeth start pushing through his gums. At around nine months of age, the big back molars come in. This hurts, so puppies attempt to alleviate the pressure and discomfort of teething by chewing on things.

- They're stressed. You may reach for a drink or a pint of ice cream when you get upset. Dogs chew. The exercise of chomping down on things makes them feel better.

- They're bored. Dogs can't surf the remote to find television entertainment or call up a buddy and pass the time, so they chew to relieve boredom.

- They think it's fun. Some dogs do love to chew more than others; this can depend on your dog's breed or individual temperament. But chewing is a very natural dog activity. Dogs enjoy it!

Dogs don't always make smart decisions about what to chew. Just because you buy your dog hundreds of dollars worth of dog toys doesn't mean that's what he'll choose to chomp if left unsupervised.

If your puppy likes to chew on items he finds around the house, a crate can keep him safe.

Electrical cords, toxic plants, and even wallpaper can sometimes appeal to a dog.

Even an innocent-looking item can cause serious danger. For example, pantyhose can be deadly—all it takes is one knee-high to cause an intestinal blockage requiring emergency surgery.

Although it can be a hassle to replace your things, you can never replace your dog. There will never be another dog like the one you brought home—he's one of a kind! A crate can help ensure your dog stays away from dangerous objects and remains a part of your family for years to come.

Visitors

Do you have friends or family who don't love your dog as much as you do? Maybe your Aunt Matilda is allergic. Maybe Uncle Fred doesn't appreciate dog kisses. Perhaps your neighbor's toddler is too fragile to handle your exuberant pup. Or maybe it's the other way around, and the toddler can't be trusted around your dog.

Crate Training: Making Confinement Fun for Your Dog   39

If your dog needs to spend the night in a kennel, he will find the experience less frightening if he has been crate trained.

What if you have a professional making repairs or additions to your home? The satellite dish installer, the remodeler, the electrician—none of them will want your dog underfoot and possibly getting hurt. It can be hard to handle your dog and company at the same time, so put Fido in his crate with a special toy, like a Nylabone, to keep him out of trouble.

Vet Visits

Hopefully, your dog will never have to spend the night at the veterinarian's office, but what if he does? Your veterinarian is not going to let your dog have the run of the clinic all night. He will need to stay in a kennel. If your dog is not used to being confined, it may upset him, and if he's sick in the first place, the added stress will just make him feel worse. Some dogs become so afraid that they even hurt themselves trying to get out of a kennel. A crate-trained dog will find this experience less frightening.

What if your dog has to be confined at home for health reasons? Your toy breed could get an infection, and the veterinarian might ask you to keep your dog still for two weeks while the antibiotic does its work. Your giant breed may suffer a serious sprain, and the veterinarian may say that he needs to stay off his leg for a couple of weeks. How can you possibly make sure your dog stays still? A crate is the best prescription!

Keeping Crates Kind

While some people are skeptical about putting their dogs in crates, some can go in the other direction. They find that crates are so good at keeping a dog out of the way that they start to depend on them too much. This can become a vicious cycle. The dog becomes more and more hyper because he's not getting enough exercise, so he acts absolutely crazy when let out of the crate. When the owners can't handle him, they put him back in the crate, where his pent-up energy just percolates some more.

A crate is meant to complement your dog's life, not consume it. Dogs need plenty of exercise each day. If you have a sporting, working, terrier, hound, or herding breed, you may be surprised to find out just how much exercise these dogs really need. They were originally bred to hunt, to chase and kill pests, or round up hundreds of sheep. Just because you don't pursue any of those activities with your dog doesn't mean his genes shut off. Your dog still has that desire built into him. (That's why a Golden Retriever puts everything in his mouth, why a Jack Russell Terrier chases the cat, and why a Border Collie rounds up every tennis ball within 10 miles.)

You need to channel your dog's energy and give him an outlet for his genetic cues. If you don't, there's a good chance your dog will develop behavioral issues, such as barking excessively or destroying your house. As many trainers say, a good dog is a tired dog! A brisk walk around the block is not enough. Neither is letting a dog live in the backyard all day; most dogs will run around a couple times, then

Crates and Punishment

A crate should never be used for punishment. If you yell at your dog and toss him in the crate when you're angry, he'll learn to associate the crate with bad things. You want him to learn that his crate is a safe den.

curl up and wait for you to come home. Your dog needs cardiovascular exercise each and every day, especially if you have an active breed. Consult your veterinarian about how much exercise your companion needs.

Training for Confinement

Training for confinement will help teach your dog to enjoy his crate for longer periods of time. You will need to practice these steps when you are home. It's a good idea to teach Fido to be crated when you're home, anyway. There may be times when you simply can't supervise him enough and he would be safer in his crate. And if you only crate him when you're gone, he could start associating you leaving with his crate and learn to dread it instead of enjoy it.

If you have a puppy less than four months of age, you've probably already had to crate him overnight or if you had to leave the house. This is fine—just use these exercises to help him associate positive things with his crate.

If your dog is behaving while confined in his crate, praise him and give him a treat through the crate door.

Passing the Time in Peace

If you have a puppy over four months of age, and especially if you have an older dog who has never been crated before, be sure your dog will happily go into his crate and stay there for short periods of time before proceeding with these steps. Please don't try and go too fast, or you will undo all of your efforts.

Step 1

Cue your dog to "Go to kennel" (or whatever cue you've

chosen) and give him a cookie or a food-stuffed rubber toy and praise when he goes into his crate.

Wait a few minutes and then walk by his crate. If he is behaving and not whining, pawing at the crate door, or barking, then praise him and give him a treat through the crate door. If he is acting up, then just ignore him and walk on past.

Step 2
Repeat Step 1 at random times, gradually working up to longer periods of time in between treats. Your dog will learn that good things happen when he's in his crate. After about ten minutes, if your dog is not acting up, open the crate door. (Don't forget to be calm and not overly praise him for getting out.)

Step 3
Gradually work up to longer periods inside the crate.

Tip:
Start with "regular" treats for the first couple passes by the crate, then work up to really tempting treats. If you start out with your dog's regular kibble, then gradually work up to chicken or liver, your dog will learn the longer he's crated, the better the treats he receives will be! Also, it's important to vary your dog's toys. If you only give him a food-stuffed toy in his crate when you leave, he could start associating that toy with you leaving, and consequently not like it anymore.

Polishing the Cue
If Fido is now happily running into his crate when you give the cue and staying there for appropriate amounts of time, you are ready for these next steps. If not, then go back to your previous steps and build up to this point.

Step 1
Now it's time to stop using a cookie to lure your dog in his crate.

Instead, stand by the crate. Give him the cue "Go to kennel!" and point to his crate as if you have a cookie in your hand. This is not to fool your dog. Dogs have an incredible sense of smell, and yours will know that you don't have a treat in your hand. Instead, what you are doing is using the same hand signal you've actually been teaching your dog all along. Dogs learn body language much faster than verbal language. As a result, if you use your hands in this way, your dog will better understand what you want of him.

Step 2

As soon as your dog goes in the crate, praise him. Shut the door and quickly get a treat from where you keep them and give it to him through the crate door. This will teach your dog that you may not always have treats with you, but he should still do what you ask because he'll be rewarded.

Step 3

Gradually move farther and farther away from the crate as you give your cue "Go to kennel."

A crate is not a babysitter. It's not meant to replace your affection and attention or to keep a dog apart from your family and its activities. A dog is a pack animal who looks to you for companionship. He needs your dedicated time outside the crate to meet his emotional needs. The crate is a tool you can use to make your life easier, but never lose sight that it needs to be good for your dog, too!

Crate Training:
The Easy Way to Housetrain

Dogs who are not housetrained and who have the run of the house will eliminate all over the place. After all, eliminating waste is a natural behavior—all dogs have to do it. They're just following nature's call, and they have no idea you want them to eliminate outside unless you teach them. Unfortunately, what you think you are teaching them may not be what they're learning. For example, you can put down newspapers or "wee-wee pads" with every intention that your dog will potty on them. But from your puppy's perspective, you are giving him some fun toys to shred to pieces. When you let your dog outside, you intend for him to eliminate outdoors. But he could be thinking it's a great opportunity to chase butterflies or bark at the dog next door.

Controlling Elimination

Crates give you better control over when and where your dog eliminates. Start with a crate just big enough for him to stand up, stretch out, and turn around in. You don't want to use such a large crate that your dog feels comfortable urinating in the corner. As he learns better bladder and bowel control, he will earn more freedom.

Learn how to teach your dog what you want, and communicate in terms he can understand.

Begin With Confinement

A crate can significantly help your housetraining program, because most dogs will not eliminate in their dens. You will need to confine your dog whenever you can't watch him like a hawk. Puppies, especially, can be like lightning when it comes to having accidents in the house. Every time they eliminate in your home, you're giving them a chance to practice that behavior. And practice makes perfect! Your goal is to give him more opportunities to eliminate outside your house with the help of the crate.

A crate can help you with your housetraining program, because dogs usually will not eliminate in their dens.

Set Up a Realistic Schedule

Review the information on setting up a realistic schedule based on your individual dog. When it comes to housetraining, I recommend feeding your dog scheduled meals rather than leaving food out all day. What goes in your dog on schedule comes out on schedule. If your dog eats food all day, he'll have to eliminate all day.

Feeding your puppy scheduled meals will help you establish a regular house-training routine.

Talk to your veterinarian about a good feeding schedule for your dog. In general, puppies less than six months old work well with three meals a day, and adult dogs work well with two meals a day. Just put the food down for about ten minutes, then take it back up again if there's any left over.

In doing this, your dog will soon have to eliminate around the same times every day. You'll be able to build his potty breaks around this routine. A schedule can also help you keep track of your dog's health. If you see your dog is urinating or defecating more than usual, you'll be able to alert your veterinarian.

Aim for Consistency

The more consistent you are in your housetraining efforts, the faster your puppy will learn. If you send mixed signals, you are likely to confuse your puppy. For example, if you put down newspapers or potty pads, you're teaching him it's okay to sometimes eliminate indoors. And if you stretch out on the floor with a cup of coffee and the Sunday paper, you can't get mad at him if he urinates all over your sports section. In short, it's much easier for your puppy to understand housetraining if you keep the rules simple and stick to them.

It's also important to be consistent with your crate schedule. If your puppy is not housetrained, leaving him loose at night is just asking for an accident. Stick with the program and you'll enjoy long-term success.

Crate Training and the Puppy Mill Puppy

 If you bought a puppy mill puppy, you may have a greater housetraining challenge. A puppy mill has lots of dogs, usually of different breeds. The dogs are kept in kennels, and the puppies are not raised inside with families.

The reason puppy mill puppies are so difficult to housetrain is because they never leave their cages. They have no choice but to eliminate in there, so they learn it's fine to eliminate in their dens. Puppies are also removed from their mothers too early. Mother dogs clean their puppies; if a puppy does not have his mother to teach him to be clean, he won't learn. These dogs learn early on that it's okay to live in their mess because they have no choice.

For this reason, I don't recommend crate training these dogs. You'll just come home to a mess. Instead, consider training your small or toy-breed dog to use a litterbox. If you don't want to use a litterbox, or if your dog is way too big for you to even consider it, then get an exercise pen or enclose a safe room with baby gates for your dog to be confined. Put a box with sod and grass in it in a corner, away from his water bowl and bed. If you get some of his urine or feces and put it on the sod, it will encourage him to eliminate in that spot. Using grass will make it easier to understand the concept of eliminating outside.

Be extra patient. You can train this type of dog … it just takes more time.

Outdoor Housetraining

When training your dog to do anything, it's important to reward him immediately for behavior you like. This means you're going to have to go outside with your dog so that you can reward him for eliminating outside the second he does so. If you wait until he comes inside afterward and praise him then, you're really praising him for coming in the door. Here is how to train your dog to go outside to potty:

If you are training your puppy to eliminate outdoors, allowing him to potty indoors may confuse hom.

Step 1

Attach a leash to your dog. If you're not attached to your dog, you can't control the environment, so he could end up running all over your backyard.

Hide a couple of small treats in your hand. Make sure it's something he really likes.

Step 2

Take your dog outside. You can put a cue on this, such as "Wanna go outside?" If you use the same cue every time with the same action, your dog will learn to associate the two.

Watch your dog for signs he has to eliminate, like sniffing the ground, assuming the position to go, etc. As soon as he starts, give him your cue to potty. ("Go potty!" or "Do your business!") Use whatever you want, just make sure you use the same cue every time.

When your dog is finished, praise him. Give him the treat and tell him he's wonderful.

Tips:
Know that puppies often have to go twice. So Fido may eliminate in one spot and then walk around a bit and go again.

Give your dog an allotted amount of time to find the right spot. If you want him to learn to do his business within five minutes, then only give him five minutes. Be consistent. Don't give him 30 minutes one Saturday and then get frustrated when he takes 30 minutes on Monday morning.

Step 3

If you want Fido to now play in his fenced yard, take off his leash and give him another cue, such as "Go play!" By making sure he potties first, you will teach him to get it out of the way before his playtime. This comes in handy especially when traveling or on bad weather days when he can't play outside.

If your dog does not go within your allotted time, bring him back inside and put him in his crate for 15 minutes. Then try again from Step 1. If he's confined, he will be less likely to have an accident in the house. If you're able to watch him very carefully, then you can do that instead.

It may be tempting to skip some of these steps, but doing so may result in a dog who is not completely housetrained. If you really want a dog who only eliminates outdoors, you have to carefully and consistently teach him that behavior. Your patience and persistence will pay off!

Crate Training:
Traveling in Safety and Style

Do you ever travel with your dog? Well, a crate could become your favorite item to pack! It will help you experience a variety of new adventures together.

Car Rides

Your dog should never be allowed to ride loose in your car. Just as everyone in your family wears a seatbelt, your dog should also be restrained for safety.

Dogs don't understand safe driving concepts. Let's say you're driving along peacefully and Fido suddenly sees another dog in a car passing by. He could lunge across you to bark at the other dog, causing you to lose control of the vehicle.

A more common danger is from outside forces causing an accident. How many times have you had to hit the brakes or swerved your car because of another driver? If you're in an accident, your dog will become a projectile in your car, and he could easily go through a windshield. What if you're hurt and unable to tell emergency personnel that you had a dog in the car in the first place? They wouldn't think to look for a lost dog.

Others have learned this lesson the painful way, so please don't repeat their mistakes. Always confine your dog in your vehicle. A lap is not a safe place for a dog to ride. Put your dog in his crate, and secure the crate using your car's seatbelt or bungee cords to hold it steady.

Flying With Fido

If you want to take your dog with you on an airline flight, keep in mind that there are strict rules for transporting pets. Be sure to check with your specific airline to make sure you don't get a rude surprise when you arrive.

Keep your dog safe when traveling by car by putting him in his crate.

Your dog will most likely need a health certificate—some airlines require one within a certain time frame of your travel dates. There may also be age restrictions on how old your dog must be before allowed to travel by plane.

In general, the only dogs who can travel in the cabin with you (other than service dogs) are ones who can fit in an airline-

What if Your Crate Is too Big for the Car?

 Some people just don't have room in their cars to easily accommodate a crate. If your car is just too small, it doesn't mean you have to sacrifice your dog's safety. Instead, use a canine seatbelt.

There are a variety of canine seatbelts on the market; they look like harnesses. Make sure you purchase the right size for your dog, as well as one that will be comfortable.

If you have passenger-side airbags in your vehicle, don't secure your dog in the front seat. An airbag can kill a dog if it deploys, so keep your dog safe in the backseat.

approved carrier that can fit under the seat. Some airlines have restrictions as to how many dogs can travel in the cabin on a flight, so make your reservations early.

Larger dogs will need to travel in the plane's cargo area in an airline-approved crate. There are specific rules about how to prepare the crate for travel, so be sure to go over them carefully.

Also keep in mind that some airlines won't transport dogs via cargo in extreme hot or cold weather for their safety. There may also be different rules for snub-nosed dogs (Bulldogs, Pugs, Pekinese, etc.), because they have a harder time breathing and are more susceptible to extreme weather conditions. Check the calendar and your destination to better plan for your dog's comfort and safety.

You'll also need to check your flight connections. Try to minimize layovers and work closely with airline representatives to make sure your dog has sufficient food, water, and potty breaks.

If you are shipping your dog via plane and not traveling with him, research common delays and issues with your chosen flights. Work with airline personnel to have backup plans in place in case of flight cancellations or problems with connecting flights. Keep in touch with the person set to greet your dog so there's no confusion about when to pick him up once he arrives.

If your dog must travel in cargo, most airlines require plastic crates. If you can take your dog in the cabin with you, some airlines have approved soft-sided carriers. Again, always check with your specific airline to make sure your crate will be acceptable. Be sure to crate train your dog before he goes on his trip. Traveling can be stressful, and if he's already used to his den, it will reduce his stress and comfort him during the adventure.

At Your Destination

If you're visiting a place that's strange or stressful for your dog, his crate will be the one familiar thing in his new surroundings, which can be very comforting.

Maybe you're visiting family for the holidays, and the place is overrun with people of all ages. Even if your dog loves the action, he

If you can take your dog in the cabin with you, some airlines have approved soft-sided carriers.

Quick & Easy Crate Training

Hotels

Some hotels don't allow dog visitors, but some may be more inclined to let Fido stay if you can prove he's crate trained. By bringing your crate, you're letting the hotel know your dog is used to being confined. You're also ensuring the hotel room will be in good condition when you leave, because your dog won't be running around tearing the place up.

If you have to leave your dog behind in a hotel room, be sure to put him in his crate. Keeping your dog in his crate is just extra insurance that he'll be safe and secure when you get back to your room.

could get overwhelmed by the activity at times. A stressed dog may react by having housetraining accidents, chewing, hiding, or even growling or snapping. Make sure your dog gets some restful crate time so he can enjoy your visit, too.

Crate Training for Travel (Car)

It's best if your dog is already used to his crate and enjoys it before you travel with him for long distances. This is why it's important to plan ahead and train your dog before your trip.

To get your dog used to traveling in his crate in the car, try these steps. They can be especially helpful for those dogs who develop carsickness. If your dog is one of them, see if your veterinarian recommends motion sickness medication for your dog. In the meantime, practice these steps to gradually introduce your dog to car rides.

Step 1

Put the crate in the car and secure it.

Give your dog his cue "Go to kennel!" (or whatever cue you chose) and encourage him to get into the crate if he's big enough to jump

Crate Training: Traveling in Safety and Style   55

into it. (You may have to lift puppies who are too small or who aren't used to jumping.) If you have a small dog who can't make the jump, just lift him into the crate. When he gets in, praise him and give him a treat.

Practice getting in and out of the crate a couple times until your dog is comfortable with the exercise. If this is a piece of cake, you can continue to the next step. If your dog is still unsure, then work on this until he's comfortable before proceeding.

Step 2

Cue your dog to get in his crate. Praise him and give him a treat when he gets in. Take a short drive around the block. When you return home, let your dog out of his crate. Gradually work up to longer trips.

Tips:

If your dog is one who will get stressed in the car, it may help to practice these steps with two people. One can drive, and the other will be in the backseat with Fido, giving him occasional treats for riding nicely in the car. Make sure you don't give him treats for barking, whining, or acting up.

Practice putting Fido's leash on him before he exits his crate. It's important he be safely attached to his leash before he hits the ground running.

If your dog does get carsick, use a toy and praise instead of treats so as not to upset his tummy even more.

Whether your dog will only take an occasional trip or whether he is one who will tag along on your every adventure, keep him safe and train him to be comfortable with traveling. That way, you'll both be happier on your journeys.

Quick & Easy Crate Training

Crate Training Challenges

A ny time you teach a dog anything, you're going to run into challenges. This doesn't mean you're a failure or that your dog will never learn. Just try to figure out what went wrong, and try to improve your training. You can do it!

The following are some common challenges in crate training.

Q: My dog doesn't seem to like his crate. He cries and whines when I put him in there.

A: There could be several reasons why your dog does not enjoy his den. First, you may have gone too fast in your training. Your dog should happily enjoy each step before you proceed to the next one.

Just back up to a step where he was successful and try again—this time more slowly.

Also, consider where his crate is located. Is it near the family? Dogs who are left alone feel left out. Sometimes just moving the crate to a place of family activity can help ease your dog's stress, so he won't feel a need to whine.

Put your dog's favorite toys in the crate, and make sure you're not using the crate for punishment. This will teach him the crate is a bad place.

It's also important not to leave your dog in his crate longer than what is reasonable. Remember, a young puppy will need frequent potty breaks, and a puppy less than six months of age is not likely to hold his bladder and bowels for eight hours. He may whine and cry because he doesn't want to soil his den. If you have a very active dog who is not getting enough exercise, he may also whine or cry because he has too much pent-up energy.

Q: When I reach for the crate latch, my dog throws himself at the door. It's obnoxious!

A: Freeze. If you let your dog out of his crate when he's acting obnoxiously, then he'll learn that's what it takes to get out—not a good lesson.

Just do nothing. Your dog will have to stop acting like a maniac sometime. The second that he does, immediately reach for the door again. He will probably start barking again. Just freeze again. He'll soon learn that if he's barking and pawing at the crate door, your hand never moves. He's smart … you just have to be smarter!

Q: My dog likes his crate fine, but he urinates on his blanket every day.

A: First, make sure your dog is not in his crate longer than reasonable. If your schedule is realistic, then remove the blanket. Some dogs will

If your dog urinates on his blanket and you have set forth a reasonable potty schedule, take it away until he learns to avoid soiling his den.

urinate on a blanket, ball it up in a corner, and stay dry the rest of the day. This is not teaching them to avoid soiling their den.

Rather than doing dog laundry every afternoon, just take away blanket privileges until your dog better understands the crate training concept.

Q: I crate my dog all day and he does fine. But at night, I want him to sleep with me. Sometimes I wake up and there's urine on the floor. What can I do?

A: Crate your dog until he's completely housetrained. If your dog is having accidents in the house, then he's not ready for that much freedom yet. It doesn't mean he won't earn it eventually, but you are just setting back your training by allowing him to take a potty break when you're fast asleep and can't catch him in the act. You're actually teaching him that it's okay to urinate in your bedroom.

Set your dog up to succeed. First, train him. Then you can have a bed buddy if you wish!

Q: I tried crate training before, but I think after reading this I made some mistakes, and now my dog doesn't like his crate. I want to try again…how do I start?

A: It may help to buy a different kind of crate. Your dog already associates the old crate with unpleasant things, so if you start with a crate that looks completely different, it could help. It also may help to put the new crate in a different part of your home—anything to make it seem new and not remind him of old experiences.

Start crate training from scratch. Make it a very positive experience, and follow the steps I've outlined in this book. Just because your dog didn't like a crate before doesn't mean he can't learn to like one now. Be extra patient with him and make it fun.

Q: My spouse thinks crates are cruel. How do I convince her otherwise?

A: Share this book with your spouse. Of course, whether or not to use a crate is completely up to you. But also know that it is cruel to set expectations for your dog that he can't possibly reach. Young puppies, for example, can't hold their bowels and bladders all day. Adolescent dogs will chew things. Leaving these dogs loose in your home is setting them up to fail. You're just asking to come home to a mess and much frustration. Why do that to yourself? It's much better for the entire family to keep realistic expectations, teach your dog what you want him to learn, and manage his environment so he can succeed.

Q: I know I'm supposed to confine my dog when I can't supervise him. But what if he's too quick and has an accident inside anyway?

A: If you catch your dog having an accident, use a stern voice and tell him, "No!" Immediately put on his leash and follow the outdoor training program. Reward him if he finishes outside. When you bring him back in, don't yell at him all over again. He may think you're yelling at him for coming back inside the house.

Never use your hands or a rolled-up newspaper to punish your dog. This will not teach him to stop eliminating in the house; it will just teach him to be afraid. Dogs who are fearful may growl or snap, so you will have an aggression problem in addition to a housetraining problem. Punishing your dog can also cause him to hide when he eliminates.

Be sure to clean the mess with a pet enzymatic cleaner, available in most

If you catch your dog having an accident inside, immediately put on his leash and take him outside.

pet stores. Regular cleaners will not hide the smell from your dog, who may return to the spot to repeat her performance.

Accidents happen. Renew your commitment to watch your puppy more closely, and be consistent with your housetraining program. He'll learn!

Q: How will I know when my dog is ready to graduate from staying in his crate?

A: This depends on your individual dog. First, he should be an adult. Toy breed dogs are usually considered adults at one year, while larger breed dogs can take two to three years. He should also be completely housetrained, meaning he never has accidents in the house. Finally, he shouldn't be destructive or chew on anything except his own toys.

It's very important that you train this gradually. It's too hard for Fido to go from confinement to complete freedom all at once.

Crate Training Challenges

A dog can graduate from a crate when he is a housetrained adult who is not destructive and who does not chew on anything except his own toys.

Step 1

Confine your dog to a room. Calmly give him a special toy or treat as you leave, just as you would if you were leaving him in his crate. Then, drive around the block and return home to see if everything is okay.

If he does well, leave him again and drive around for five minutes. Return home and see if everything is okay.

If he does well, leave him again and take a ten-minute drive.

Gradually work up to longer times, aiming for the amount of time you are usually away from home, such as at work. This could take a couple days, or even a couple weeks. Take your time. If you come home to an accident or destruction, take steps back in your training.

Step 2

If you wish, you can give Fido more room, using baby gates to block off areas if necessary.

Every time you increase his space, follow the process in Step 1. Leave him for short times at first, gradually building up to longer times.

Index

Measurement Conversion Chart

1 gallon = 3.7854 liters
1 inch = 2.54 centimeters
32°F = 0°C (water freezes)
75°F = 23.9°C

CONVERTING FAHRENHEIT TO CELSIUS
Subtract 32 from the Fahrenheit temperature.
Divide the answer by 9.
Multiply that answer by 5.

Photo Credits

Photos on pages 37 and 59 and on front cover (bottom right) and back cover courtesy of Mary Bloom.

Photos on pages 17 and 54 courtesy of Paulette Braun.

All other photos courtesy of T.F.H. archives.